SUNDAY STORIES

Everyday Lessons

Fay Quanstrom

WestBow
PRESS®
A DIVISION OF THOMAS NELSON
& ZONDERVAN

WestBow Press books may be ordered through booksellers or by contacting:

WestBow Press
A Division of Thomas Nelson & Zondervan
1663 Liberty Drive
Bloomington, IN 47403
www.westbowpress.com
1 (866) 928-1240

ISBN: 978-1-5127-6913-5 (sc)
ISBN: 978-1-5127-6914-2 (hc)
ISBN: 978-1-5127-6912-8 (e)

Library of Congress Control Number: 2016920996

Print information available on the last page.

WestBow Press rev. date: 2/1/2017

CONTENTS

A WORD FROM THE AUTHOR

The stories in this collection honor Jesus's method of incorporating objects and events of everyday life into his teaching.

I believe that Bible texts connect in practical ways to everyday human experience, with universal truths that apply to children as well as to adults. The Harvey stories invite the reader to see through the eyes of a child. The simple tales relate to listeners of all ages, who are more likely to hang stories on their mind's hooks than to retain strictly didactic material. These stories can open the spiritual eyes of any reader or hearer to see God at work in everyday moments. They can be tools that model learning to discern God's voice speaking to the heart in common circumstances of life.

Harvey began life as the main character of children's talks, providing an example of how a given text might live in the ordinary moments of a child's life. The fact that Harvey sees life through the eyes of a pre-schooler makes him accessible to all children, some of whom relate directly to the story events and others of whom imagine themselves to know the "moral of the story" without being told.

By reading one or more of the texts that follow each story, and by using the italicized prayer, the reader can take hold of the Biblical truth that lives in Harvey's experience. Parents can ask their own questions to enlarge the learning opportunity. These might include "Has this ever happened to you?" "Have you ever done this?" "What do you think Harvey and the children in the story *should* have done or said?" A brief prayer finishes each unit. The Scripture text on which the story is built appears at the end of the page.

ACKNOWLEDGEMENTS

I was encouraged to develop these stories by Jean Czinki and Rev. Kurt Simon, of the English Congregational Church, Big Rock, Illinois. They have been told all over Illinois as well as in Arizona and London, England. This book developed in the professional hands of Jonathan Davies with encouragement of family and friends. I thank you each heartily!

DEDICATION

These stories are dedicated to Sigourney, Graham, Beckett, Itzel and Isabella, five precious grandchildren.

1—WHAT TIME IS IT?

The babysitter came early to Harvey's house. Both Mom and Dad were going away for the whole day. Harvey hoped they were going shopping—maybe for him! Harvey heard Mom say to the babysitter, "There's one important thing I want you to do—bake cookies. The dough is in the refrigerator. Just drop it on the cookie sheets and bake the cookies for tomorrow." Harvey and the sitter nodded. They liked baking cookies.

The day was going to be a good one. First they read a book. Harvey thought about the cookie baking, but they had all day. Then they ate lunch. The sun was shining, so in the afternoon they walked to the playground. They could bake when they got home. They climbed on the climbing frame, slid down the slide, and swung on the swings. Other kids were there, and they all had a great time. Harvey and the sitter stayed until suddenly they realized the sun was going down. They walked home and talked about the good day they had had. The sitter opened the refrigerator and got out the bowl of dough. They found the cookie sheets.

Just then Harvey saw the lights turn into the driveway and heard the car engine idling as the garage door went up. He was happy that Mom and Dad were home. He ran to hug them. Dad lifted him high in the air. Mom sniffed. "I thought I'd smell cookies. I left you with one job."

"Oh, we meant to do it. We were just about to start. We were so busy all day doing good, fun things. We hope you'll understand."

Help us to do the right things at the right time, Lord.
Matthew 24:45—50; Romans 13:11—14

2—Shield and Reward

Harvey and Mom went shopping at the mall. Mom said, "You'll have to hold my hand."

"Why? I'm a big boy." Mom did not say anything. They saw other kids with their parents. "Why is that boy on a leash?" Harvey asked.

"He probably won't stay close to his mom, Harvey, so she's keeping track of him that way."

Before long an announcement came over the speaker. "We have a lost child at the service counter. Will her mom please claim her."

When Harvey heard that, he held tight to his mother's hand all afternoon.

> *You want to lead and guide us. Let us hold tight to your strong hand.*
>
> Genesis 15:1

3—Finding the Way Home

Harvey played all afternoon with a friend at the friend's house. They were so busy playing that the time went very quickly. Suddenly Harvey stopped what he was doing. He began thinking about home, and Mom, and Dad. He looked out the window. He couldn't see anything. It was dark. It looked like night. Suddenly Harvey was afraid. He did not know the way home, but he did know he lived a long way away. *What was he going to do?* he wondered.

"I don't know the way home," he said out loud. His friend looked at him with a strange look. Harvey stood up. He would go and find his friend's mom. She might know what to do. He started for the kitchen, hoping she was there.

Just then he heard something wonderful—the voice of his own Mom. He ran and gave her a great big hug around the legs. Harvey knew that she knew the way home!

> *Thank you, O God, that you are with us, showing us the way home.*
>
> Isaiah 40:1—11

4—Who? Me Grumble?

Harvey's mom called him to the table for the second time. Dad was already seated.

"No!" Harvey called in his most important voice. With that, Dad lifted him into his chair and bowed his head to say grace.

The minute the prayer was complete, Harvey announced loudly, "Yuck! I hate carrots! I hate carrots! Blah! This is a yucky supper."

"Might I guess that Harvey's been playing with Lou today?" Dad ventured.

Harvey's eyes grew big. He turned and looked at Dad. Dad had been gone all day. No one had said a word about their day yet.

"Yes, he did," Mom answered.

"How did you know that, Dad?" asked Harvey. "You are really smart."

> Remind us, O God to be happy and grateful, even when others aren't.
>
> Exodus 16:2—15

4

5—Who Can Help?

Harvey and his family were driving along a busy highway with two crowded lanes of traffic going each way. Harvey's mom suggested he try counting the red cars for something to do. He began. "One, two, five, 'leven, 'leventeen, 'leven-twenty...".

Just about that time Dad said, "Oh, oh!"

And Harvey said, "Oh, oh!"

Bump, bump, bump, thunk went the car. Everyone was very quiet. Dad sighed deeply. He was all dressed up. Harvey did not think that dads dressed in suits could fix cars. Dad got out carefully, watching the traffic whiz by. "Maybe someone will stop and help us," Mom imagined and hoped, just loud enough for Harvey to hear.

Harvey began to guess which car might stop to help. His head went back and forth watching a rainbow of cars speed past. Dad had the trunk up, probably looking for a tool. No one stopped. Harvey wondered why everyone was in such a hurry when his family needed help.

Then he heard the sound of brakes behind them. A dirty-looking man in old clothes got out of a rusted pickup and talked with Dad. He knew what was wrong. Soon Harvey, Mom, and Dad were on their way. Mom said, "Isn't it interesting that with all these people in beautiful, shiny cars, the person who helped us came in a beat up car, and looked ragged and dirty too."

Thank you for helping us, sometimes in surprising ways.
1 Corinthians 12:3b—13

6—SMALL BUT STRONG

Harvey was playing at the home of a friend. They and their toys were spread out across the floor when Harvey heard tires squealing, then brakes, then a door slamming. Harvey looked up and asked his playmate, "What was that?"

"A car," answered his friend.

The floor of the house shook a little when a tall man stomped by the playroom. "Little brats," he muttered. "I could beat you both up."

"Who was that?" asked Harvey.

"My big brother. He's home from college. We don't pay much attention to him."

Harvey wasn't done thinking about that when the big brother came back toward the door. He stepped on one of the toys, and then he said some words that Harvey hadn't heard before, but he knew they must be bad words. "Those are bad words," Harvey said to the tall brother. "You shouldn't talk like that."

When the brother squealed out of the driveway in his car, Harvey's friend asked, "How did you dare to tell my brother not to talk like that? He's so big and strong. He said he could beat us up, too!"

Harvey took a deep breath and answered, "Sometimes a kid has to do what a kid has to do."

Thank you that you can make children strong, O God.
1 Samuel 2:12—20

7—Counting the Cost

Harvey decided to build the biggest possible castle. It would be bigger and better than any his friends had made. He got out his blocks and started at one end of the family room. He lined the blocks up as straight as he could, thinking about where the tower would be, and about how splendid his castle would look. In it, his action figures would rule. Around it, his toy animals would graze like sleek horses for the heroes to ride. He could hardly wait to see the finished castle.

The doorbell rang and it was Grandma. She smiled and asked, "What is this you're working on, Harvey?"

"This is going to be the biggest and best castle," answered Harvey. He explained to Grandma how high the walls would be and how round and tall the tower would be.

"That is a grand plan, Harvey! I didn't know you had that many blocks." Harvey scrunched his nose and looked into the block box. *One, two, three,* he counted to himself. *How could he finish his castle with only three more blocks?*

The doorbell rang again. Harvey's friend was there to play with him, so Mom and Grandma could talk. "Whatcha doin', Harv?"

"This is the world's biggest castle," announced Harvey, "and I'm building it for my action figures."

"That doesn't look like a castle to me! It looks stupid. Really stupid! It's just a row of blocks!"

Harvey's head drooped and he felt terribly sad. His mom poked her head into the family room. *Moms always hear bad words like 'stupid.'*

"Why don't you build a small castle for practice?" Mom suggested.

Help us to do good work, whether our jobs are large or small, O God.

Luke 14:25—33

8—Hearing and Listening

Harvey and Henry played outside in the stupendous-for-snowballs snow. They were making a wonderful fort in which to play. They rolled big balls of snow together and arranged them in a circle of snowballs. Then they started another row by putting snowballs on top of the first row. They dug down in the middle, and curled up snug and warm, out of the wind. From far away they could hear someone calling. Henry clapped his hands over his ears. He did not want to hear anyone calling, because he did not want to leave the cozy snow fort. Harvey asked, "Henry, is your mother calling you?"

Henry said, "I don't hear anything." His mittens were still over his ears. The two friends kept on playing and building their fort into a splendid hiding place in the snow.

It wasn't long until Harvey heard *his* name being called. "Harvey! Harvey!" He scrambled out of the fort and lumbered across the yard to his back door. Henry came along behind because he did not want to play alone. Harvey's mother brushed the snow off their clothes and helped them get their coats off. She had hot chocolate ready for them. It tasted so good after being out in the cold!

"Thank you for coming when I called, Harvey," Mom said. Henry looked down at the floor. Then phone rang.

"Yes, he's here," Harvey's mother said. "Yes, I'll send him right on home."

Lord, let us recognize your voice, and let us answer quickly.
Mark 1:16—20

9—Selected and Rejected

Old Auntie came to visit Harvey this week. Harvey loved Old Auntie's visits. She brought presents when she came. The presents weren't big, but they were things Harvey enjoyed very much. Once, Auntie came with a coloring book. Another time she brought a bottle of bubble-blowing stuff. Sometimes she had a small toy for Harvey. When Old Auntie came this week she had *nothing* in her hands. Harvey was disappointed. He hung around the chair where she sat, just in case she was waiting to give him a present.

"Oh, Harvey! I have something for you!" Auntie finally said. "You are going to have a choice today. There are two things in my hand. You may have just one, but you may pick either one. It's up to you! You may decide." She opened her hand and Harvey saw two shiny coins, one bigger than the other.

Was bigger better? Harvey wondered. *Bigger* looked like *more*. Harvey hesitated a moment, looked up, and smiled at Old Auntie.

"Thank you," he said as he took the nickel. Auntie put the dime back in her pocket.

Show us when bigger is not best, we ask.

1 Samuel 16:1—13

10—THE TEACHER

Harvey loves books, but he does not know how to read. His mother said that in order to read he needs to know the alphabet.

Harvey has a toy that plays the alphabet song when he pulls the string. Harvey pulled the string. *A-B-C-D-E-F-G*. Harvey pulled the string again. *H-I-J-K-L-M-N-O-P*. And again! *Q-R-S, T-U-V, W-X-Y and Z*. Then he picked up a big book. He would be able to read now! He opened a book and began at the top of the page. Aloud, he said, "O-N-C-E-U-P-O-N-A-T-I-M-E." Harvey knew the letters, but he did not know any words yet.

"I need a teacher!" Harvey said in a loud voice.

"Yes, you do," his mother agreed. "Soon you will go to school, and you will have a teacher who will help you learn how the letters make the words, the sentences, and the whole stories."

Harvey skipped away, found his alphabet song toy, and gave the string another pull.

O God, we need you as our teacher. Let us learn from you.
Mark 1:21—28

11—EVIDENCE

Harvey was hanging around the kitchen with Mom, when he heard her say, "Oh, oh! We have a mouse!"

"Where? Where?" cried Harvey. "I want to see the mouse!"

"The mouse isn't here. I don't *see* the mouse, Harvey. I only see the evidence. Look at these teeth marks. A mouse has been here."

"Evidence," said Harvey. "Evidence," he repeated, as he watched Mom set a trap.

At the table that evening, Dad said, "There were some serious skid marks near the corner tonight. I'm sure they weren't there this morning."

"That's *evidence!*" exclaimed Harvey.

"You're exactly right. From the evidence we know that something happened, even though we didn't see it happen. The evidence was left behind," Dad said.

> *You have left evidence, Lord, of your life and death. Thank you for the way the evidence points to you. Help our faith in you to grow, we ask. Amen.*
>
> John 20:18—29

12—MOUNTAIN TOP

Harvey and his mom were sitting on the couch looking at pictures.

"Oh, look! Look how I've grown. I'm much bigger now!" Harvey exclaimed. "Here is our trip to the mountains. The mountains were beautiful."

Harvey studied the picture of his family on the mountain, looking out at other mountains in the distance. *What a special day that had been*, Harvey thought. "Do you remember asking why we couldn't live on the mountain, Harvey? You thought that was the place we should build a house! Then we could stay there all the time, at the best and most beautiful spot in the world. Would you like to see another picture that's old, Harvey?"

Mom went to the shelf. She ran her finger along the edges of albums. She finally found the one she was looking for. She brought it back to Harvey, opened it, and turned the pages until she found the picture she was looking for. "Here! Here I am with Grandma and Grandpa at the same place in the mountains. We took a picture there, too, on a trip we made together long ago. What a special place! We felt so close to God there."

> *O God, you give us a glimpse of yourself and your splendor from time to time. Help us to worship you and learn about you. Help us to remember who you are—our Savior and our God.*
>
> Mark 9:2—8

12—THE COOKIE DOUGH MONSTER

Harvey was helping his mom make cookies. He pushed his chair up to the counter. He watched the flour, sugar, eggs and butter go into the bowl. Mom mixed them together into a smooth dough. Harvey knew these would be very special cookies when Mom put in a whole bag of chocolate chips. *The dough looked so good*, thought Harvey. His mouth watered. He could not wait. Mom turned to get out the cookie sheets. Harvey quickly dipped his hand into the bowl. He began to lick the dough from his fingers.

"Harvey! We don't do that!" Mom said with her sharp voice. "You know you shouldn't put your fingers into the cookie dough."

"Sorry," he answered, as he hung his head.

Then Mom said, "This *once* I'm giving you a spoon of cookie dough."

Harvey could hardly believe it. He smiled, took the spoon, and opened his mouth very wide. He clamped it over the whole spoon and squished the sweet dough onto his tongue. He could feel the chocolate chips in his mouth. He could let them melt slowly, or he could chomp them down. He chomped, and the dough, and the chocolate chips were gone. Harvey thought about how good that spoon of dough had been and how much he loved chocolate chips. In front of Harvey on the counter sat the mixing bowl, half full of dough. Mom turned to take the first cookies from the oven. Quickly, Harvey stuck his hand into the bowl for another taste. Mom was very cross when she saw what Harvey had done. "Harvey," she said in the voice that Harvey knew was used for very important words, "you said you were sorry for doing that very thing. If you really *are* sorry you don't do it again. You stop doing what you are sorry for."

Suddenly the cookie dough didn't seem so good. A tear rolled down Harvey's cheek. "I won't do it again, Mom. I really *am* sorry."

Dear God, so often we find ourselves doing the same wrong things. We want to stop. We need your help, and ask you for it.

1 Peter 3:10—12

13—TAKING ACTION

Harvey was playing in his yard. He heard a door slam, and his friend on the other side of the street came out his door. Harvey waved. His friend waved back. "Whatcha doin'?" his friend asked.

"Playing," answered Harvey. "Wanna play with me?"

"Sure." And with that, Harvey's friend dashed into the street. Loud squealing of brakes filled the air. A car seemed to have come out of nowhere! The car stopped just in time to keep from hitting Harvey's friend. Harvey's mom dashed out of the house without her coat, even though it was coat weather, when she heard the sounds on the street. She grabbed Harvey, hugged him, and checked that he was okay. The other mom had come running too, when she heard the sound of brakes. She picked up Harvey's friend, and said very sternly to the driver, "You must slow down on this street. Be careful."

"I'm really upset," the other mom said to Harvey's mom.

That night at the table, Harvey's mom began the story of what had happened that day by saying, "I'm so upset."

When Dad heard how fast the car had come, and how Harvey's friend had nearly been hit, he said, "If you're upset, you should do something to keep this from happening again."

The next day Harvey's mother started talking with other people who lived on their street. Before long, workers came to install a sign. It said, "Slow, children at play." Harvey watched as the workers put it in place.

"This should make this street safer," the worker announced to no one in particular. Then he looked right at Harvey, and he said, "But you've got to stop and look both ways, too."

> *Thank you, God, for watching over us. Help us to obey the rules you give us for life.*
> Exodus 20:1—17; John 2:13—22

14—FAILURE?

Harvey went to visit the country cousins. Cousin excitedly described something, and finally persuaded Harvey to follow, and see for himself. "It's a chicken! She's going to have babies! They are in the eggs now, waiting to come out! Come and see!"

Harvey knew that chickens don't really have babies, but he was still curious. He and Cousin ran across the lawn to the place where mother hen had her nest. As they caught their breath, Cousin's face turned from an excited smile, to surprise, and then disappointment. Hen was gone! There were no chicks. "Look! Broken shells. Empty shells," Cousin squealed.

Harvey saw nothing warm, or fluffy, or yellow, but he could see that Cousin was very sad.

They ran back to tell Auntie the bad news—no hen, no chicks, only broken shells. Auntie listened to the excited, disappointed Cousin and Harvey. Then she took their hands and said, "Let's go. I would like to see what you are telling me about."

The three of them went back outdoors together. Cousin and Harvey were right. There was no hen or chicks, only broken shells. "Just a minute," said Auntie. "I think I hear something. Look over there! There's hen *and* chicks! They left behind what they didn't need—broken, empty shells."

Harvey and Cousin watched the little chicks, fluffy and yellow, pecking at the ground, and they smiled.

> *Lord, out of our emptiness and brokenness you make all things new. Thank you.*
>
> John 19:38—20:8

15—WHO SAID?

Harvey busily picked up a stick and carried it to another spot in the yard. Then he found two more. He put them on top of the others, making a little pile. Harvey kept on finding sticks, and putting them on his pile. A voice called from the house behind Harvey's, "What are you doing, Harvey?"

"Picking up sticks."

"Why?"

"'Cause my dad said."

"Why?"

"My dad said to."

Just then Mom called for Harvey. She said something softly to him. Harvey nodded. He left the stick project and moved toward the flower bed.

"Why are you doing that?" the boy called across the yard.

"Mom said!" Harvey answered. He picked a bright yellow daffodil.

"What are you doing?" called the boy.

"Picking flowers," answered Harvey. He picked another and another.

"Why?" asked the boy.

"Mom said I could." And with that Harvey headed for the back door, through the mud, with a big bunch of flowers in his hand.

> *Lord, you give us the power to act in your name. Let us hear your voice and do what will honor you.*
>
> Acts 4:5—12

16—Tree Trimming

Harvey was out in the yard, watching Dad work. He wanted to help, but Dad said he would have to watch. Helping on this project was too dangerous.

"What are doing?" Harvey asked when Dad started the chain saw.

"I'm going to trim the trees," Dad answered.

"Why?" asked Harvey. "I like them the way they are."

"These branches hang down and make it hard to see out the driveway when we're backing the car up. The driver needs to see if the way is clear, and that will be easier with these branches gone."

"I see!" Harvey answered. He listened to the saw's whine and watched the branches fall down. "What's next?" Harvey asked when he got back from carrying branches to the spot Dad had pointed out.

"I'm cutting these branches off with the pruning shears to give this tree a more attractive shape," Dad explained. "Then we'll take a look at the apple tree. It needs pruning so that it will bear fruit instead of just a lot of leaves."

"The trees will be better when we men get this work done," Harvey announced.

> *Your trimming in our lives is for our good and God's glory.*
> *Help us remember that, Lord.*
>
> John 15:1—8

17—Commanded to Love

Harvey sat, buckled into his car seat. As his family drove, Harvey began asking what the signs said. That one says, "Watch for deer," Mom told him. Harvey pressed his nose against the window, and watched for deer, but he didn't see any.

"What does that one say?"

"Slow down!" And soon a flagger waved to send the message again in another way: *slow down, workers ahead.*

"There's another sign!" Harvey exclaimed.

"Do not pass," Dad said as they drove up the hill.

That one says, "Love one another," Harvey squealed.

Mom said, "It's really, 'Turn on headlights,' but 'Love one another' is something we should always remember, too."

> *In our lives you tell us that we must love one another. We need your help to do that, Lord, because sometimes we do not even like one another.*
>
> John 15:12

18—Christ the King

Sometimes people call Harvey "Mr. Harvey." Friends call him "Harv." He doesn't like it when someone calls him "young man," because it sounds like he is about to get in trouble. Sometimes, when Harvey's mother puts him to bed, she rubs his head and calls him "my boy." All these names tell something about Harvey. "Mr. Harvey" sounds dignified. "Harv" sounds like a name for a special friend. "Young man," sounds grown up.

Harvey's teacher asked, "Did you know that Jesus had a lot of names? He was called 'Carpenter' and 'Emmanuel,' 'Light of the World,' 'Bread of Life,' 'Teacher,' 'Rabbi,' 'Savior,' 'Nazarene,' 'Healer,' 'Living Water.'"

"That's nine," Harvey spoke up.

"Let's make it ten!" his teacher suggested. "How about 'King'? Today we're talking about another name for Jesus—'King.' It takes many names to tell us about Jesus."

Thank you, Lord, that Jesus is so wonderful it takes many names to describe him.

Isaiah 9:6

19—BREAD OR A STONE

Harvey's friend, Peggy, and he were playing house. Peggy was fixing things in the play kitchen, and Harvey was taking care of the baby doll. But mostly, Harvey was thinking about lunch. "I'm hungry!" he announced.

"Lunch is ready!" said Peggy. Harvey left the baby doll and sat down at their little table. He was ready to eat. Acting very important, Peggy set a hamburger in front of Harvey. But Harvey knew that he was not going to take a bite. *That hamburger was a plastic dog toy.*

Then Harvey became cross. He really *was* hungry. He wanted *real* food. "That's no help for a hungry boy like me," he said. With that, he left the table and ran to Mom in the kitchen. She was fixing peanut butter and jelly. "That's better!" declared Harvey. "I hope you have some for Peggy, too."

Thank you that you provide real food for our bodies and our souls.

Matthew 7:7—11

20—Given to Another

Harvey and Dad had a bedtime story at the end of Harvey's busy day of playing outdoors. Then Dad said he'd like to talk. "I was thinking about how much you wanted your little bike before you got it."

"Oh, yes," said Harvey. "I wanted it more than anything."

"And you made some promises," Dad continued. "You said, 'If I had a bike I'd take care of it, and I'd ride it carefully, and I'd put it away every night'."

"And I'd share. I'd let others ride it sometimes, and I do!" added Harvey.

Then Dad said, "I'm thinking about giving it away to some kids who don't have much."

Before Dad finished the sentence, Harvey squealed, "What?" and sat straight up in bed. He wasn't sleepy anymore! "Why?" he asked, his eyes very round and wide open.

"For two days I've stepped over it in the driveway. You aren't taking good care of it. I think those other children might do better."

Oh, oh, thought Harvey, because he knew Dad was right.

Help us, Lord, to keep our promises about sharing the love
and good news of Jesus with others.

Matthew 21:33—43

21—CLUES

"We'll do something special when I get home from work," Dad told Harvey.

"What is it? What is it?" Harvey asked. He loved surprises, but waiting for them was so hard.

"I'll give you a hint, Harvey! 'White as snow,'" Dad said.

"White as snow," Harvey repeated. He put his chin in his hands and sat thinking as hard as he could. "White as snow," Harvey said again. "I can't guess! I need another hint! Please?"

As Dad went out the door, he said, "Okay, here's another clue for you, Harvey. 'Black as midnight.'"

Harvey thought, *maybe it's a newspaper. It is black and white. We're going to buy a newspaper! But that isn't very special. 'Black and white.' A zebra is black and white! Maybe we're going to the zoo! I think we're going to the zoo!*

The day seemed very long. At last, Harvey heard Dad at the door. Right away, Dad asked, "Are you ready, Harvey?"

Harvey smiled very big and said, "I think we're going to the zoo!"

"Come along," Dad said. "I'm ready, but I have to tell you, we're not going to the zoo."

"But zebras are black and white, and they live at the zoo," Harvey protested.

"'Black as midnight, white as snow, hot as summer, cold as winter.' Now what do you think it is?"

Harvey couldn't imagine. He was still wondering when he and

Dad got to the ice cream shop. Harvey looked all around, and then he heard Dad say, "Two hot fudge sundaes, please."

Harvey's eyes got very big. He looked at his sundae and said, "White as snow; black as midnight." He took a bite and said, "Hot as summer; cold as winter." He smiled as said, "Thank you, Dad."

Lord, what you tell us in your word is true, but sometimes we still do not understand. Help us, we ask.

John 14:1—3

22—Second Chance

Harvey and Mom decided to bake cookies—rolled sugar cookies. *The flour, the sugar, and the eggs made a wonderful mess,* thought Harvey, as Mom mixed them all together. When the mess turned into a white ball, Mom rolled the dough flat and showed Harvey how to cut the circles.

She turned to clean up the dishes, and Harvey went to work. He plopped the cutter down once, and again, and again. *What fun!* One circle overlapped another. *Oh well. What interesting designs!* he thought. Harvey poked at the dough with his finger and the dough squished in that spot. Then he made a great big dent in it.

About that time, Mom turned around. "Oh, Harvey! That's not going to work. We'll have to start over!" She gathered the dough into a ball and rolled it out again, as good as new. When the new circles were cut and put into the oven to bake, Mom and Harvey sat down to read a story. It was a great story, so they were having a wonderful time.

All of a sudden, Mom stopped. She sniffed air and jumped up. Harvey followed her into the kitchen. Smoke poured from the oven as Mom pulled out the pan of burned cookies. "Look at this!" she exclaimed. Harvey looked at the burned cookies. *They were no good.*

As Mom scraped the burned cookies into the garbage, she said, "Sometimes grownups need second chances too."

Thank you, that you help us to start over when we need to.
Luke 19:1—10

23—LIFE GROWS

Harvey saw flowers along the neighbor's sidewalk and he thought they were very pretty. "Mom, could we plant flowers too?"

"That's a great idea, Harvey! Let's do it this afternoon." Harvey could hardly wait. They would have flowers blooming at their house just like the neighbors did.

He and Mom got everything ready—dirt and digging tools. They decided where the flowers would go. Harvey's mom said, "Here, Harvey, open this."

She handed him a little box, not at all what Harvey expected. He thought they would have trays of plants like he'd seen outside the store. The little box had a picture of a flower on it, and Harvey thought, *Our flowers come in a little box, not a tray. When I open the box will there be flowers inside?* He pulled the top off, but there were no flowers or plants inside. He dumped out the contents. "These look like little rocks!" he said. "These aren't flowers. They're dried up. They look dead. What good are these?"

Harvey didn't know that the neighbor's flowers had looked like that a few weeks before.

God would make these dry, dead-looking seeds grow into flowers too.

Thank you that you give life to plants and people.
                                        Acts 9:36—42

24—King Who?

Harvey and his family stopped to eat as they were coming home from their visit with the cousins. Where they stopped there were crowns for kids. Harvey smiled and crowned himself. "I'm a king! I'm a king! I'm a king!" he repeated, looking very pleased.

"And what would your kingdom be like, Harvey?"

"People would share!"

"And what else?"

"People would be kind!"

"And what else?"

"In my kingdom no one would be hungry. Everyone would have a warm bed! In my kingdom no one would fight."

"You'd be a good king, Harvey."

When they'd eaten, and thrown away the cups and wrappers, Harvey crawled into the back seat so Dad could buckle him in. He was still wearing his crown for the rest of the ride home.

> *We imagine that we would be excellent rulers, Lord, but we know that you are the one and only, perfect King of Kings.*
>
> 1 Timothy 6:11—16

25—TRUE WORDS

Harvey was picking dandelions. The big boy next door, who was picking up sticks, called to him, "Hey, Harvey! Want a dollar? I'll give you a dollar if you come help me."

Harvey bounded over and picked up an armload of sticks for the stick pile. He worked and worked until he and the boy next door had cleaned up all the sticks that the wind had blown down. Then the boy went inside his house. Harvey waited and waited. While he waited he thought about the dollar he had worked for, but the boy did not come back. Harvey sadly returned home. The phone rang. It was Dad calling him from work. "Harvey, you and I are going to do something special tonight. It's a surprise."

"Promise?" asked Harvey.

"Yes," Dad answered.

On the way home from the ice cream shop Harvey kicked a stick, and then he said, "Thank you, Dad, for keeping your promises."

You are a promise-keeping God, and we are so glad that you are.

Revelation 22:6

26—Harvey's Zoo

Sometimes Harvey likes to dump all his plastic animals into the bathtub when the bath water is running. The lions and camels float alongside one another. The horse and the giraffe move side by side. He likes lining up the sheep and the dogs and cats. Sometimes he starts with the smallest animals—the mice—and arranges them along the edge of the tub to the biggest—the elephant.

Once, when the animals were all in a row, Harvey announced, "The animals are all happy. They are playing 'Follow the Leader' and tonight the mice are the leaders. They are taking turns, too."

"I think your lions might even lie down with the lambs when they stop to rest," Dad added.

"Yes, Dad, no animals are even growling tonight."

"Lions have been eating lambs for so long that grown-ups can hardly imagine anything different. I'm glad you can imagine it, Harvey," Dad said, as he handed Harvey a towel and the water started running out of the tub.

> *O God, we wait for the time that lions and lambs can lie down together.*
>
> Isaiah 11:1—9

31

27—STORY HOUR

"There's story hour at the library tomorrow, Harvey," Mom mentioned at breakfast. "Would you like to invite a friend to go with us?"

"Yes! Yes! I love story hour!"

"Who would you like to invite? Henry? You may use my phone right after breakfast."

Harvey ate his last bite of toast and wiped his mouth. He laid his napkin down and slid from his chair. "May I call Henry now? Where's your phone, Mom?"

The next day Harvey thought that it was taking a very long time before Mom was ready to leave for the library. While he waited, he thought about Henry, and how happy he was to come along with them. After a while, he thought about his friend, Penny, so he asked, "Mom, could we stop and pick up Penny, too?"

Later than morning, Mom and Harvey picked up Henry and Penny for the ride to the library. The children gathered in a circle on the floor in the reading room, and when they were all quiet, the librarian began to read. She stopped at the end of each page to show the kids the pictures. After the story, the children looked at books and each of them chose five books to check out.

When they were all in the car with their books beside them, Henry said, "That was great! I really like story hour at the library. I didn't even know there was such a thing as story hour until you told me."

Thank you for inviting us, Jesus. We know there are many who do not even know about you, and we can invite them.
Matthew 4:12—23

28—HELPING HANDS

One night Harvey's family had company for dinner. Mom was fussing around all day—cooking, and peeling, and stirring. At last the doorbell rang. Harvey ran to the door when his dad answered it. Jan and her family were there. Jan was carrying a dish covered with foil.

"Look what I have!" she exclaimed to Harvey. "Look!" She pulled back the foil. "I did this. I fixed this all by myself!" Harvey saw carrot sticks lined up neatly. At the other end of the dish celery sticks were lined up just as neatly. In the middle were olives. Harvey loves olives. "And when I finished, I got to eat the last olive!" Jane announced. Harvey's mouth watered.

"Come see this!" Harvey said as he turned toward the dining room. "See here? I folded all the napkins."

When the food was on the table, Harvey's dad said grace. "Thank you, Lord, for our friends here tonight. Thank you for this good meal. We ask you to bless the hands that prepared it."

Bless the hands that prepared it. Harvey hadn't heard anyone say that before. He opened his eyes and peeked at Jan. He thought about her hands arranging olives and carrots and celery. He thought about Mom peeling potatoes this afternoon. He looked at his own two hands and smiled.

Thank you for hands with which to work and play.
Matthew 26:17—19

29—JOBS

Harvey's mom said it was time for Harvey to learn to make his bed. This was his new job and he was to do it every day—smooth the sheets, pull up the covers, and put the pillow just so. It made Harvey feel good and grown up to do important work like this.

If this is my job, thought Harvey, *maybe I should get pay. Dad gets pay for his job.*

So Harvey said to Mom, "Maybe it would be good if you paid me to do my job. Ten cents a day would be fine."

Mom smiled. "Some jobs we do just because we're part of the family, Harvey."

> *Help us to remember that we are serving you because we are your children, and we love you, O God.*
>
> Galatians 6:1—6

30—To Save You

Harvey's mom asked his dad to fix the door of the tall cabinet, so the men—Harvey and Dad—began by checking it out. Dad said, "You stay here. I'm going to get a screwdriver. Don't touch anything."

Harvey waited and waited for a long time. He wondered what the problem with the door looked like and decided to see for himself. *I will just step on the cabinet shelves and take a peek*, he thought. So he put one foot on the bottom shelf. He reached up, took hold, and raised his other foot. Things started to move, to fall, and just at that moment, Dad came around the corner.

"Harv....eeey!" he screamed as he lunged for the cabinet. Bang! The cabinet hit Dad's head. Crash! A glass vase fell and broke, cutting his arm. A big knot swelled on Dad's head, and his arm was bloody, but he had caught the cabinet.

Harvey had not been squashed because Dad had caught the cabinet when it fell. Harvey was very quiet and stayed out of the way the rest of the afternoon. At bedtime Dad came into Harvey's dark room. Harvey whispered, "I'm sorry, Dad. I'm sorry that I disobeyed and did wrong. Why did you hurt yourself like that?"

"I love you, Harvey." And Dad gave him a big hug.

Lord, you took what we had coming, what should have fallen on us, and we know it hurt you. Thank you.
Isaiah 53:4—6

31—Loving One Another

Harvey and his friend played happily all morning. They had peanut butter and jelly, and apples for lunch. After lunch they sat looking at books, each with a different book in his lap. They began to squabble over whose book had the best pictures. Harvey grabbed at his friend's book. The friend hung on tight. "I want to see it!" Harvey demanded.

"It's mine!" squealed his friend. "Give it to me!"

Dad walked into the room. Harvey ran as fast as he could to Dad and jumped into his arms. He hung on as tight as he could. Just then the doorbell rang. Friend's mom was at the door. Harvey's friend ran toward his mom. Harvey whispered, "I love you," to his dad. Then, looking over Dad's shoulder at his friend, Harvey made the worst face he could, before he stuck out his tongue.

When his friend and his mom had gone, Mom said, "Harvey, you can't love Dad and be mean to your friends at the same time. It just doesn't work that way."

Lord, help us remember that loving you means loving others. Amen.

Matthew 5:21—37

32—THE GIFT

Grandma visited at Harvey's home. After the wonderful days that Harvey and Grandma had, she returned to her own home. She called to say she'd had a safe trip. "May I talk with Harvey?" she asked.

"How did you like what I left you?

"I don't know, Grandma. I didn't know you left me anything." By the time Harvey hung up, he was busy with something else. Later, Mom was changing the bed and vacuuming in the guest room. Harvey's present sat on the dresser, unopened.

"Harvey!" Mom called, but Harvey was so busy coloring that he answered, "I'm busy," and did not come to see why she had called his name.

It was as though Grandma hadn't left a gift at all, because Harvey hadn't opened it.

> *You gave the gift of Jesus, O God, but we must accept him*
> *in order to complete the gifting.*
>
> Romans 5:12—21

33—BORN ANEW

Harvey visited with Mom to see a new baby. He thought the baby looked so tiny and so pink, only about so-o-o long. *How could a real person be so small?* he wondered.

On the way home he asked, "Was I that little when I was born?"

"Oh yes, Harvey, and very pink! You've grown up so big!"

Harvey sat up very tall and smiled. He said to himself, *So big! I'm growing so big.*

> *O God, you make all things grow. We want to grow, with your help, into people who love you with all our hearts.*
>
> 1 Peter 1:18—23

34—OUR SUBSTITUTE

Harvey, Mom, and Dad had lots of errands. They parked at the mall and went first to the bookstore. Harvey found a great book, and Dad bought for him. Harvey was all smiles. He proudly carried the package. Next they looked at shoes. They found just the right pair to wear for playing. Then Harvey carried *two* packages. Mom found the things she needed, and carried them in several bags. Dad had his own stuff. They walked and walked. The mall seemed enormous to Harvey. The stores seemed very far apart. Harvey's packages seemed heavier and heavier. "Dad, could you please carry my shoes and my book? They are so heavy."

Even though Dad carried Harvey's packages, he thought, *This is getting to be a very long shopping trip.* "How much longer, Mom?" he asked.

"Just a few more stops, Harvey. You can do it." Harvey kept walking, but he was going slower and slower. Finally he stopped.

"My legs don't want to work anymore," he said. "Could you please carry me?"

Dad lifted Harvey into his arms. Mom took the bags with Harvey's shoes and book. Harvey napped all the way home. When they pulled into their driveway, Harvey woke up. "We're home!" he announced.

They talked about their day and their big shopping trip after they went inside. Harvey hugged his dad and said, "Thank you for being my legs when I didn't have any today."

When our strength is gone you carry us, Lord. Thank you.
Isaiah 53:1—6

35—God Comes Back

Harvey and his parents went for a drive. Harvey wondered where they could be taking the flowers. He did not think they were going to visit friends. Out in the country, they came to a winding road. They slowed down and turned into a cemetery.

"Here! This is the spot!" Mom said. They got out of the car, took the flowers, and walked through the grass that was just beginning to turn spring green. "This is where my grandma is buried," Mom explained. "She was your great-grandmother," she said to Harvey.

Harvey looked at the stone and rubbed his hand along the carving. "Great-grandmother," he said softly. Mom read what was carved into the stone—Great-grandmother's name, the day she was born, and the day she died. They laid the flowers by the stone. As they began to walk back to the car, Harvey looked around at all the grave markers. He called out, "Look how big *this* stone is!"

"Oh, that's the stone of an important man, an inventor from our town. Important people often have large markers."

"Let's look for another important person!" Harvey suggested. "Let's look for Abraham Lincoln!" Harvey was thinking about Abraham Lincoln because Dad had shown Harvey a picture of him on some money just the day before. Harvey was sure that a person had to be very important to be on money.

"Abraham Lincoln isn't buried here, Harvey."

Harvey tried to think of someone else important. Then in a loud voice, he said, "Jesus! *He's* the most important of all! I want to see Jesus's marker."

"Jesus doesn't have a grave marker, Harvey. Jesus is alive! He rose from the dead. First, he died for us, but he rose again. That's the good news of Easter."

> *Thank you for the good news of Easter, O God, that Jesus is alive.*

Matthew 28:1—10

36—WHAT'S YOUR NAME?

Harvey and his cousins were playing together because their family was celebrating Mother's Day at Grandma's. It was a lovely day, so the cousins played outside. "Stay out of the mud," the grownups said sternly.

"We better not get muddy," the cousins said to one another.

Harvey had an idea! "I know what we can do! Here's a stick. I'm going to poke it in the mud, but I'll stay out of the mud."

Everyone found a special, long stick. They were having fun poking their sticks in the mud, just like Harvey said. Pretty soon they were flipping little globs of mud, even getting some on their heads. Harvey stopped. He felt very important with his stick. He held it proudly, stood up very straight, and announced, "I am Harvey Hanson!" It sounded good. "I am Harvey Hanson," he repeated.

The girl cousin copied him. She stood tall and said very loudly, "I am Heloise Hanson."

Harvey looked at her. He was ready to say, "I said it first," when the littlest cousin stood next to Harvey and Heloise and said, "I am Thomas Hanson."

Harvey asked, "Is your name really Thomas Hanson? Heloise is Hanson. I'm Hanson. You're Hanson. We all have the same name!"

With that, they ran as fast as they could to Grandma's back door. They were in such a hurry that they barely wiped their feet. They ran in to the grownups and Harvey cried, "Guess what! We have the same name!" He pointed at the cousins and announced,

"Harvey Hanson, Heloise Hanson, Thomas Hanson. We do! We have the *same name!*"

The grownups looked at one another and smiled. "Your dads have the same father—Grandpa Hanson." And out the door the cousins went to play some more.

Remind us, O God, that as Christians we share the same name.

Acts 11:21—26

37—GRANDPA'S CANDY

Harvey was hunting for something in his room. He looked everywhere in his closet. It wasn't there. He searched on the shelves. It wasn't to be seen. He looked behind the door. It wasn't there either. He looked in the drawers, but still found nothing that he was looking for. He *did* find something else—a little package of candy that Grandpa had left for him. Grandpa had said, "Save this for later," and Harvey had done just that. He'd saved it so long that he had forgotten all about it until this moment. And now he had forgotten what he'd been looking for in the first place.

He sat, plunk, on the floor and looked at the candy. It was his very favorite. He opened the package and smiled. He popped the first piece into his mouth and remembered how Grandpa had pushed him on the swing. He ate the second piece and thought about how he sat in Grandpa's lap while Grandpa read him stories. *Grandpa loves me*, thought Harvey. *I think Grandpa is thinking about me right now!*

> *You love and remember us, Lord, and we remember and love you.*
>
> Luke 22:14—20

38—Walking and Talking

Harvey had been snuggled into Mom's lap while she was reading. They came to the end of the story and Mom said, "Hop down, Harvey. I've got to get dinner ready."

Harvey threw his arms around his mom and said, "You're the best mom in the whole world! I love you." He slid to the floor and climbed into his little rocking chair. He rocked, and rocked, and he said a little rhyme—"Rock and talk and walk. Talk and walk and talk and walk."

"Harvey, go wash your hands," Mom said from the kitchen.

Harvey kept on rocking and singing, "Talk and walk and rock and walk." He loved the way the words kept time with his rocking.

"Harvey! Wash your hands!" Harvey kept rocking and talking.

"Harvey! Walk right over to that sink! A boy who loves his mom does what she says."

Lord, may our walk match our talk, every day.
Matthew 21:28—32

39—We Can Pray

Just after breakfast Harvey's mom's phone rang. As soon as she said hello, Mom said, "Oh no!" Then she asked a lot of questions. "Really? When? Where? Should I come?" Harvey wondered what was wrong. When the call was over, Mom said, "Grandpa is in the hospital. It's his heart."

Harvey thought, *Grandpa is so big and strong that he can lift me high over his head. He can tell the best stories. He can even drive a truck!*

Then Harvey saw Mom wipe her eyes. She was crying! Harvey didn't think moms and dads cried. *Weren't they too big to cry?* He did not want Mom to be sad. That's when Harvey said, "Mom, we can pray."

"Oh, Harvey, that is exactly what we need to do."

"Dear God," Harvey prayed, "please help Grandpa's heart, and help Mom not to be sad. Amen."

"Amen," Mom added as she hugged Harvey tight.

Thank you for answering our prayers and healing our hurts, and our hearts.

Matthew 9:9—13, 18—26

40—NAMES

Harvey ran as fast as his legs could carry him, jumped as high as he could into the air, and landed in the pile of leaves his dad had raked. The smell of fall surrounded him as the leaves rustled around him.

He caught his breath, brushed his arms and legs, and plunged into the pile again. *Fall is wonderful!* thought Harvey. Dad moved around to the side of the house, but Harvey stayed to play in the big pile. Just then, he could hear some of the older boys laughing and talking as they headed toward him on the sidewalk. When one of them caught sight of Harvey, he pointed at him and began to laugh. "Look at him! He's so little!"

"And that shirt! Ugh-l-e-e-e!" added another.

"His legs are so short he can hardly run. Ha! Ha! Ha!" "You're funny looking, kid. And we don't like you, either."

Suddenly, Harvey felt cold and sick inside. *Where was Dad? Dad would protect him from the bullies.* Harvey ran to Dad, and Dad, who had heard it all, picked him up. "I think it's time for some hot chocolate," Dad announced.

As they sat with their steaming cups of cocoa, Dad said, "It hurts when people call you names, doesn't it? I used to hear that same stuff—'short,' 'stupid,' 'funny looking,' and more. Grandpa had sent me to the corner store when I was hardly bigger than you, and I was walking home with some milk. Kids passed me, laughing and talking so mean. It seemed like their cruel words made the glass milk bottle too heavy to carry. I set it down and it broke. I ran home, crying, and your grandpa held me while I talked about it."

Harvey smiled. Dad understood. He was safe in Dad's lap.

> *Lord, thank you for holding us close when we hurt. You know what life on earth is like for us. Keep us, for Jesus's sake.*
>
> Revelation 7:9—17

41—God's Word, our Light

Harvey and his friend were playing. Things weren't going as well as they usually did. Harvey felt cross. He reached over, quick as a wink, and pinched his friend. A howl went up. When Mother heard the commotion and what Harvey had to say about it, she gave Harvey that certain look and said, "The Bible says, 'love one another'," Harvey looked sheepish. He told his friend that he was sorry, but a few minutes later they had another squabble.

"I want it."

"Give it to me!"

"I had it first!"

Harvey's friend took a deep breath and announced in his loudest, almost-shouting voice, "The Bible says, 'obey your neighbor'!"

Once again, Mother appeared. "The Bible doesn't happen to say 'obey your neighbor'," she chided, "but what's the problem here? Maybe it's time for a snack."

When his friend had gone home, Harvey had a question for his mom. "How did you know that the Bible doesn't say 'obey your neighbor'?"

"You have to read it, and study it, Harvey. That's the way to know what the Bible says."

Help us to read and study your word, and to do what it says.

Psalm 119:105

42—Choices

Harvey went to Sally's birthday party. He had counted the days until Mom would drop him off with a present at his friend's house. Finally, it was party day! At the party Harvey found a lot of peanuts during the peanut hunt. He did not do as well with musical chairs, but he did laugh a lot when the music started, and especially when it stopped. Harvey had never been to such a special birthday party! The party even had two different kinds of cake! He could not decide between white and chocolate. Sally's mother said he could come back for more if he'd like. *Yes!* thought Harvey.

When the chocolate piece was demolished, he was still hungry for cake. The white piece that he chose had a big, frosting rose on it. Harvey's mouth watered as he ate it, and the ice cream, and some more peanuts. Everything was so-o-o good! He was just thinking about running his finger along the cake plate to collect another frosting flower when he heard his mother at the door.

Harvey talked all the way home in the car about the wonderful party. He was not at all hungry at supper. In fact, his tummy had started to hurt. The hurt seemed to grow, until it became a very bad tummy ache.

"What was it that you ate at Sally's party?" Dad asked. "*Two* pieces of cake? *And* peanuts? *And* frosting flowers?"

Harvey thought he could feel the frosting flowers blossoming in his tummy right then.

"It sounds as though your choices caught up with you, Harvey."

Lord, help us to make the right choices, because our choices matter.

Matthew 25:1—10

43—Meant for Sharing

Dad returned from a business trip with a surprise for Harvey. It was a small square box with a beautiful lid. When Harvey opened it, he saw four of the most perfect and prettiest chocolate candies he had ever imagined. A layer of cellophane covered them. He looked at them, put his nose down on the cellophane, and sniffed the chocolaty fragrance.

"Thank you," he said to Dad.

These are so special, he thought. I *will save them. They are the best.* Harvey went to his room and looked until he found the perfect saving place. It felt special to be able to save chocolates instead of eating them right away. The longer he left them in the perfect saving place, the easier it was. Sometimes he'd get them out and just look at them, but mostly Harvey forgot about the beautiful, little box of perfect chocolates.

Sometime much later, Grandma and Grandpa visited. After dinner someone said, "It's a shame we don't have some chocolates."

Oh! thought Harvey, *I have my special, beautiful box of chocolates.* He ran to his room and pulled them from their safe place. He hurried back and gave the little box to Grandma. Grandma smiled. Harvey could tell that Mom was very pleased that he would share. Grandma took a piece and bit into it. Grandpa took a piece and bit into his, too. A funny look came across their faces. They quit eating.

"I don't think these are good anymore," Grandma said. Harvey looked at Grandpa. He had quit after one bite too.

"Some things aren't meant for saving," Dad said.

Help us to honor you, God, by sharing the things that should be shared.

Matthew 25:14—30

44—Remembering

Harvey's house was busy. Harvey and his parents were getting ready for important company. Harvey's mom said, "Harvey, don't talk with your mouth full. Close your mouth when you're eating. Mind your manners. You know about being polite." Harvey nodded his head.

When the doorbell rang Harvey looked with wide eyes. He thought to himself, *this is what important people look like.*

Soon Mom called everyone to the table. Harvey sat on his own chair and the company sat at the sides of the table. Mom was at one end, and Dad at the other.

The important lady smiled, reached for the basket of rolls, helped herself, and passed them to the next person. The important man picked up the butter dish and passed it. Harvey thought about manners. He looked at Mom, and then Dad. He suddenly said what he was thinking. "Aren't we going to pray?"

The important man and woman got quiet and sat very still. They looked at Mom and Dad.

Dad said, "Harvey, you may pray."

Harvey closed his eyes very tightly. He folded his hands and prayed, "Dear God, thank you for hammers and for food. Amen." He opened his eyes. The important man was smiling. So was the important lady. Harvey did not know why they would laugh at the end of a prayer.

Dad said, "Thank you, Harvey. I'm thankful for hammers, too."

Help us, O God, to be thankful for all good things in our lives.

Deuteronomy 8:7—18

45—LOOKING FOR WALDO

One night Harvey had a babysitter. When the babysitter, Kim, came to Harvey's house, she brought a book with her. After Mom and Dad left, she said the book was called *Where's Waldo?* Together they looked at the pictures. The pictures had lots of people in them, and lots of things to look at. Harvey especially liked the pages that showed machinery. He looked and looked for Waldo on each page. Sometimes he could find Waldo all by himself. Sometimes Kim gave him hints. "Where's Waldo?" they asked again and again. "There's Waldo!" was the answer.

Soon it was time to get ready for bed. Harvey brushed his teeth, put on his pajamas, and climbed into bed. Just then, Harvey heard Mom and Dad come home. Mom took Kim home while Dad came in to say "goodnight" to Harvey, and to pray with him.

"Where's Waldo? We found Waldo," Harvey said. "Where's God? That's what I want to know. Where's God?"

"God is everywhere," Dad answered.

"I don't see God everywhere. I don't see God at all."

"God is invisible," Dad said. "God lives in the hearts of those who love God, Harvey."

Dad patted the covers in place. "Good night, Harvey."

Harvey's eyes began to close. Softly, he said to himself, "Where's God? God is everywhere. God is everywhere."

We may not see you, but we know you are everywhere, including with us at all times. Thank you, Lord.
Psalm 139:1—12, 23—29

46—LOVE

Harvey was playing in the yard and he invented a new game—
Dandelion Football! He ran across the yard and kicked a fluffy
dandelion head. He turned and ran toward another dandelion.
He kicked and smashed it to pieces. He kicked another, extra
hard, and then another. His shoe turned yellow from Dandelion
Football.

"I love this game," Harvey said to himself.

He heard Mom calling from the back door. "Harvey! Come in!"

Harvey called back, "I love you," and ran to kick another
dandelion.

"Harvey!" Mom called.

"I love you, Mom," Harvey answered. He wanted to kick
every dandelion in the yard. There were lots more dandelions that
needed kicking.

"Harvey! Now!"

Oh-oh, thought Harvey. *That voice means that the Dandelion
Football game will have to stop.* Harvey ran toward the door, kicking
one last dandelion on the way. "I love you, Mom," he said once
again.

"Harvey, when you love someone, it makes a difference in what
you do. You do what the one you love asks you to do."

When we say we love you, Lord, let us do what you ask
—to care tenderly and regularly for others, for your sake.
1 John 5:1-3

47—Nicknames

Harvey was hanging around the kitchen, scuffing his foot on the floor. Mom stopped to take a good look at him. She could see something was wrong, and asked, "What's the trouble, Harvey?"

"The kids are calling me a name, and I don't like it," Harvey answered.

"Oh?"

"The other day somebody was teasing me, and they said that I blushed. Someone yelled, 'Look, he's all pink! He's pink!' Now everybody's calling me 'Pink.' It was only one time that I blushed. It's just not fair."

"You're right! It *isn't* fair. I had a nickname when I was a girl. The kids called me 'Freckles.'"

"You don't have freckles, Mom!"

"I used to. They seem to have faded now. Dad went to school with a fellow they called 'Shorty.' He was the tallest one in the class!"

"That's funny," Harvey giggled.

"Nicknames are funny in that way. People aren't trying to be mean, but words and names can hurt."

Dear God, help us to be understanding and kind to others. You know our real names. We call you by your name, Savior. Amen.

John 20:19—29

48—Costly Love

"Grandma, please tell me a story about the olden days," Harvey asked.

Grandma smiled. "Do you mean a story from when I was about your age?"

Harvey nodded his head.

"That wasn't the olden days, Harvey, so I'll tell you a story that *my grandma* told me. That gets a little closer to 'olden days.' My grandma's family had chickens that ranged freely around their farmyard. One big hen was a special pet that Grandma called 'Clucky.' She got that name because she often sat on her nest, clucking importantly. Sometimes the eggs in her nest hatched! One hot summer day the wind was high. Grandma had just had a cool glass of lemonade when someone yelled, 'Fire!' Dry grass and stubble at the edge of the farmyard burned quickly. The wind pushed the fire across the prairie. Grandma's family beat the flames with wet burlap sacks and rugs. Grandpa plowed a firebreak ring around the buildings. The smell of fire, smoke, and the heat of the flames filled the air. Finally, the fire was out and Grandma's family sighed and hugged one another. They were all safe. They were tired and dirty, but safe. The next day Grandma walked with Papa to check the pastures. As they went along, Papa occasionally turned debris over with his foot. Grandma and Papa both jumped in surprise when he kicked over a mound and revealed a nest of chicks, fresh and yellow, ready to scurry about. That was Clucky's nest! That burned mound was Clucky! She died in the fire, but under her wings her chicks were safe and alive!

Harvey's eyes grew wide as he imagined the fluffy chicks hiding under Clucky while the fire swept over them. He felt sad that Clucky died.

Then Mom said, "Grandma always said that Clucky made her think of Jesus, who died in order to save us."

Yes, thought Harvey, *that is what Jesus did.*

> *When we remember that you died for us, we are so thankful!*
>
> John 3:1—17

49—The Mission

"Would you like to go for a ride, Harvey? I'm going on an errand."

Harvey ran out of the house and let the door slam behind him. He loved to ride with Dad. He buckled in and away Dad and Harvey went on a ride. When Harvey looked out the window, he announced, "I've never been here before."

"That's true," Dad answered, "but we're not that far from home." Dad stopped the car by a doorway. He rang the bell and waited. Harvey pressed his nose against the window. The man who came to the door looked friendly. Harvey heard Dad say, "We brought some clothing that we thought you could use."

"Oh, that's great!" the man said. "We can use clothing here at the mission. Many of our guests need something to wear. We can use gifts of money, prayer, and volunteers, too," the man said.

"We're glad to help," Dad answered.

"Would you like to look around the mission?" the friendly man asked. Harvey and Dad followed the guide down the hallway.

"That man needs a bath," Harvey observed. Dad squeezed Harvey's hand and quickly gave him that look that means, *be quiet.* They went on to the dining room, the workroom, the chapel, and the sleeping quarters on their tour.

"Thank you for letting us see the way you're helping people," Dad said as they left. "We'll be praying for you and the mission's work. I'd like to help by volunteering, too."

Bless the people who help others at places like the mission, Lord.

Matthew 25:31—40

50—What Shall We Do?

Harvey went to a birthday party. He knew he was at the right house, even though he had not been there before, because there were balloons outside. He carefully carried the present up the sidewalk to the door of his friend's house. Other kids arrived and the party was about to start when the telephone rang. The mom said that she would have to leave for a little bit. Then she said, "Boys and girls, these two young people are in charge while I'm gone. Do what they tell you to do," and she left.

One teenager said, "Okay, kids. Let's decide what we're going to do."

The other teenager announced, "We're going to take a vote."

One of the children asked, "What's a vote?"

"It's your pick of what to do. Raise your hand if you want to go outside." Only a couple of boys raised their hands.

"Okay. How many want to play 'Button Button'?" Two girls raised their hands. The teenagers looked at one another. "How many want to play 'Duck Duck Goose'?" No one's hand went up. "Oh, forget it," said the boy teenager. "Just do whatever you want."

Some kids played with dolls and some looked at books. Some chased one another. Some sat down. One boy with a loud voice said, "This is a weird party. I don't know what to do."

Just then, the mom came back. Harvey wondered what would happen next. She blew a whistle, and said very loudly, "Quiet! Two lines! Make two lines! Boys here. Girls there. Boys, into this bathroom to wash your hands. Girls, go upstairs. Wash your hands. Then we'll have birthday cake."

When Harvey was riding home, he told Mom about the party—the vote, the kids just doing whatever they wanted, and the mother's whistle. "I like home best of all," Harvey said.

Sometimes we just don't know what to do, Lord, and we need your help.

Psalm 37:1—9

51—COOPERATION

Harvey's teacher announced that the children would be going on a field trip to the aquarium. The teacher passed out a notice that listed all the rules for the trip. Mom or Dad was to sign the permission slip at the bottom of the page. "When everyone goes by the rules for the trip, we will all have a better time and be able to see more of the aquarium," the teacher said.

At home, Harvey's parents read him the rules for the day. There were more rules than when the class stayed at school. Mom and Dad said the rules were important to remember, and follow. *That is the same thing that the teacher said,* thought Harvey.

On the day of the trip, teacher read the rules one more time. She explained why everyone needed to do his or her job of staying together, listening, and paying attention.

That day Harvey and his friends remembered to do all the things that the teacher had talked about. They stayed together with their group. They listened to the guide. They talked softly. And most of all, they looked at all the fish.

When everyone was back on the bus, Harvey's friend turned to him and asked, "Did you see those kids who were running wild and had to leave before lunch?"

"Yes," replied Harvey. "I'm glad our class cooperated. We got to stay so much longer and see so much more."

> *Help us each to do our jobs, whatever they are, so that we can all be happy together.*
>
> Nehemiah 10:23—24

52—God Provides

Harvey's mom told him to gather his things, because they were going to visit an old friend. Harvey put his coloring book and some crayons into his bag. He found his little bear and some books, and put them into the bag. He set the bag by the door. He was ready to go! In a few minutes Mom and Harvey were out the door. Harvey sat in his car seat, all buckled up. They backed out of the garage, turned down the drive, and were on their way. Mom turned on the radio and was humming a song that Harvey had never heard. He looked out the window and wondered when they would get to the old friend's home.

"O-oh!" Harvey said all of a sudden. "I forgot my bag and all my toys by the door!"

"I'm sorry," Mom said, "You'll have to get along without your things."

When Harvey and Mom arrived at the friend's house, he was very glad to hop out of the car. Mom and her old friend hugged one another. The friend said that Harvey was getting to be a big boy. Harvey already knew that, but he smiled.

Sitting on the chair in the living room, he swung his feet as he listened to the ladies talking. He looked around the room. There were no toys anywhere. He went outside. There was no swing set, no bike, and no sandbox. He came back inside, and said, "I don't have anything to do."

Mom's friend said, "I can fix that! Come along!" In the kitchen she found a brown paper grocery bag. She cut it along the side and took off the bottom. She laid it flat, folded it once, twice, three times. "Here's an empty book for you, Harvey!" she said. Then she took some flour and mixed it with water. "This will be your paste," she announced. "In your book you may paste pictures. You may cut them from this magazine. Here you go."

Harvey sat at the kitchen table. He went to work cutting out the prettiest pictures he could find, and then pasting them on the pages of his book. He knew this would be a great book. When it was time to say good-by, Harvey thanked his mom's friend, and carefully carried the book to the car. He could hardly wait to tell Dad how Mom's friend had made something out of nothing.

Dear God, open our eyes to see the ways you provide for us, making something from nothing.

Mark 6:30—44

53—DISCIPLESHIP

Harvey and his mom took a ball with them to the park. They sat near the playground equipment and looked at all the children playing. Every swing was full. The teeter totters were full. The merry-go-round was full. Harvey and Mom decided to play catch.

Harvey counted each toss of the ball, "One. Two. Three." Back and forth the ball went between him and Mom. "Four. Five. Six." Some of the children were tired of waiting for a turn. Harvey could tell they were getting cross. "Seven. Eight. Nine." Mom and Harvey kept tossing the ball back and forth. "Ten. Ten and one. What's after ten?" Harvey asked.

"Eleven," Mom called out.

Harvey stopped and held the ball. He could hear mean words, words that Mom said you should never say. The biggest boy was pushing littler kids. Harvey dropped the ball and ran to the edge of the chips around the swings. "You shouldn't talk like that. Those are bad words," he said to the big bully.

With that, the big bully swaggered over to Harvey. "Get out of here, little brat. Scram. I hate kids with big mouths. Get lost." Harvey's eyes grew very big. He wondered why anyone would scold him for telling the truth.

> Please help us to be strong about doing and saying the right thing.
>
> Ephesians 4:15

54—COMPARING

Harvey was playing outside when he saw something moving in the grass. It was a frog! It came hopping toward him. "Hi," said Harvey.

"Hi," croaked the frog. At least Harvey was quite sure that that's what he heard.

"My name is Harvey," Harvey said.

The frog looked at him and blinked. Harvey did not know what to say next, but he blurted out, "I'm bigger than you!"

Frog looked at Harvey. Then he stretched out and stood on his hind legs, much taller than Harvey. Harvey stood as tall as he could, but he was not as tall as Frog.

"Well, someday I will be taller than you, even when you are on your tip toes. I'm going to grow as tall as my dad."

> O God, we often measure ourselves against each other. Help us to be growing and growing, measuring ourselves against you.
>
> Ephesians 4:1—3, 14—16

55—MERCY

Harvey sat on the steps at his back door, just looking around. He could see the big boys next door doing something together. They were looking intently, then rushing ahead, squealing. "There it is!" "Over there!"

"Where?"

"There!"

Harvey's eyes got very big. *What is where?* he wondered. He squinted and looked extra hard. The boys were chasing something, trying to catch something. Then Harvey saw that they were after a big, green frog.

The frog hopped into Harvey's yard. Harvey could hear it making a sound with each hop. "Mercy! Mercy!" it seemed to say.

Harvey looked at the big boys. "Why are you chasing the frog?" he asked.

"None of your business, little kid," they answered, and they kept on leaping after the frog, trying to catch it.

"Mercy! Mercy!" Harvey heard the frog croak as it hid under the shrubs. Harvey hoped the frog would be safe there.

Harvey went inside. He asked Mom, "What does 'mercy' mean?"

"That's a hard one, Harvey. I'd say 'mercy' is a mixture of kindness and love."

> *Lord, may our lives show others your mercy, that special mixture of kindness and love.*
>
> Ephesians 2:4—10

56—NEW FRIENDS

Harvey was at church, looking around and looking around. He could not find what he was looking for. Finally, he decided to ask, "Where's that nice man who was always here?"

"He's gone. He moved away."

Someone else added, "We said good-by to him last week."

Harvey hung his head. He felt very sad and very lonely.

That was when the butterfly came along. The butterfly lit on Harvey's shoulder. He was sure he could hear it say, "You need to be making new friends all the time, Harvey. I'll be your friend."

Help us to be a friend and to make new friends so we can share Jesus's love with others.

Acts 2:43—47

57—A Place at the Table

It seemed as though everyone at Harvey's house was busy getting ready for company. Mom did not have time to play or to talk, but Grandma did, so Harvey crawled into Grandma's lap with a book. She began reading to Harvey. Suddenly Harvey asked, "Grandma, do you want to see me write my name?"

"Of course, Harvey! I didn't know you could write your name."

Harvey found a pencil and paper and climbed back up beside Grandma. He set the paper on the book they had been reading. Then Harvey squeezed the pencil very tight, and made a line on the paper. "A long one," he announced. He drew another line and said, "Another long one. And then a line across. That's an H."

Grandma smiled. "That's great, Harvey! Let's see the rest!"

"That's all I know—two long ones and the one across."

"Would you like me to do the rest?" Grandma asked.

Harvey nodded, and Grandma made the letters a-r-v-e-y. Seeing his whole name made Harvey very happy.

"I'm hungry, Grandma."

"Why don't you find your place at the table, Harvey. We're fancy today, with a place card for each person. Look for your name."

Harvey climbed up on a chair to look. "No H," he said, and he climbed down. He climbed up on the next chair. *Still no H.* Harvey began to wonder if there was a place for him. *Maybe I will have to sit in the high chair like I did when I was little.* He climbed up to the next chair, and he saw his name—H-a-r-v-e-y! He was so happy that he stayed on the chair, in his place, right there, until dinner.

When everyone else came to the table, Dad looked around at each person. "Everyone's here. Let's join hands and thank God for our food," he said.

And that's what they did!

Dear God, you have made a place for each of us. We are grateful.

Mark 14:12—26

58—WHO ARE WE?

Harvey came into the kitchen with his blanket. He asked Mom to fasten it around his shoulders. Mom used two big safety pins, and pinned the blanket in place.

Then Harvey spread his arms, and began running from one room to the next. "I'm Batman!" he squealed. He ran into the kitchen, and as he passed Mom, he called, "You're Robin!"

Harvey wasn't supposed to run in the house, but Mom thought he was so cute that she let him do Batman, with his blanket cape flying behind him. All afternoon he was Batman. He was still Batman at supper.

"Who do we have with us tonight?" Dad asked Mom. "Oh, Batman's here tonight."

"And that's Robin," Harvey announced, very seriously, as he pointed to Mom.

"Batman, you're going to need to eat your peas," Dad reminded. "Robin, may I please have some more potatoes?"

When Mom tucked Harvey into bed that night, she said, "Good night, Batman."

But when morning came, Harvey was Harvey again.

Dear Lord, help us to remember who we are and who you are.

2 Corinthians 5:17—21

59—First Fruits

Harvey's mom bundled him up because it was chilly out. Then she and Harvey and Dad drove down their street, past all the places Harvey usually went, and out to the country to pick apples. Harvey loves apples.

When they saw a sign with a big red apple on it, they knew where to turn. At the orchard they decided to pick a whole bushel of apples. Dad helped Harvey carry the basket to the right tree. "Is this the tree with the best apples on it?" Harvey asked.

"I'm sure it is. Just look at them," Dad answered.

Harvey reached as high as he could to pull one of the best apples off the tree. He put it into the basket. Then he decided to make a pile of apples from those that had already fallen to the ground. Mom and Dad kept picking. The basket filled quickly. When it was full, they carried it to the car.

"May I please eat one on the way home?" Harvey asked.

"How about this extra-red one?" Dad said as he put a beautiful apple into Harvey's hands.

At home, Mom started to make a pie. Harvey wanted to help, but Mom thought his job should be finding the biggest apple, so he looked and looked until he found the very best, biggest one.

Mom said, "Harvey, you do good work."

At bedtime Harvey set his biggest and best apple on the table by his bed. He crawled under the covers. Dad came in to say bedtime prayers with Harvey. "Thank you, God, for apples," Harvey prayed when it was his turn.

Dad kissed Harvey goodnight and said, "I love my little apple picker." When Dad was gone, Harvey lay in his bed thinking about apples. He thought about the wonderful smell. He thought about rubbing the apples on his clothes to make them shine. He even thought about taking a bite out of the biggest and best apple by his bed right then.

Then Harvey had an idea. He crawled out of his warm bed, picked up his biggest and best apple, and walked quietly down the hall on his toes. He peeked into Mom and Dad's room. It was dark and quiet. He crawled onto their bed, right between Mom and Dad. "I brought you a present, Dad. I love you." Then Harvey gave the biggest and best apple to his dad.

> *From your bounty you give to us, Lord. Let us be generous in giving the best back to you.*
>
> Mark 12:41—44

60—A Plate Full

Harvey went to Penny's birthday party. The children ran in the yard, and played games, and had a wonderful time. Then it was time for refreshments.

Harvey loves refreshments. He looked at the good things on the table. First, he put a hotdog on his plate. Next, he saw red jello! He loves red jello, so he served himself a big spoon of red jello. He saw a big pot of baked beans. Yum! He piled them on his plate. On top of the hot dog, the jello, and the baked beans, he put a big handful of potato chips. His plate was full, heaping full!

"Where shall I put the cake, Harvey? Do you have room for cake?" Penny's mother asked. Then she answered her own question. "I don't think you do."

Harvey's plate was so full that no room was left for the best treat of all, birthday cake.

O God, you have provided so much for us. Let us not miss out on the best that you give. Amen.

Mark 10:17—22

61—TRANSFORMED

Harvey pushed a chair over to the counter and crawled up on it. That was hard work, but he wanted to see what was happening. He wanted to see what Mom was doing.

He looked into the bowls on the counter. *Gray stuff. Brown stuff. Cold Stuff.* He wanted to say "yuck," but he knew he would be in trouble if he said that, so instead, he asked, "What *is* that?"

"Leftovers," Mom said. "I'm going to make supper out of them."

Yuck, Harvey thought. *I do not think that I will be hungry for supper.*

He decided to go and play in his room. He found a paper bag, and began drawing and coloring on it.

"Come to the table!" Mom called in a few minutes. Harvey pulled the paper bag that he had been coloring over his head. *Maybe he could be a stranger tonight.* As he stumbled toward the table, Harvey wondered, *how could Dad thank God for the stuff he'd seen when he was standing on the chair that afternoon?*

Harvey didn't say anything when Dad put food on his plate and his own. Dad looked happy, and helped himself to a fork full. "What is this, Mom? It's really tasty!"

Mom smiled. "Chef's Delight," she answered. Harvey did not know what "Chef's Delight" was. He had never heard of it, and was sure he would not like it, because he had never tasted it before. "Well, really, 'Chef's Delight' is leftovers. I transformed them."

Chef's Delight. Harvey carefully ate a very small bite. Then, he tried a medium-small bite. Harvey decided that "Chef's Delight" was actually okay, maybe even good.

After supper Harvey went back to his room. He looked around and spotted a toy that he had not seen or played with for a long time. He moved the parts and changed its shape. Then he carried it proudly out of his room to show Dad. When Dad saw it, he nodded. "See! I transformed it," Harvey announced. "I transformed something, too. It's called 'Harvey's Delight'."

Lord, in a world with so much change, help us to see you. Change us. Remake us. Transform us in the way that pleases you. Amen.

Romans 12:1—2

62—GIVING

Every time Harvey goes to Sunday School, his mom or his dad gives him money for the offering. "If you didn't give me money, I wouldn't have anything to give," said Harvey one day. He stopped to think for a moment. Then he asked, "Does Grandpa give you money for your offering?"

"No, Harvey."

"Then, where do you get it?"

"God gives me good health and the ability to work at my job. I earn money by working. But all that we have really comes from God. That's why we give back. It's a way to say 'thank you.'"

"You can say something to God without using words?"

"Yes, you can. There's a saying, 'Actions speak louder than words.'"

"That must mean that if everyone puts something in the offering, everyone is talking at once!" Harry observed.

> *We say we love you, Lord, when we give our tithes and offerings.*
>
> Mark 12:38

63—Good Gifts

Harvey was playing with his yellow dump truck. He made engine noises as he pushed his way into the kitchen, his back end higher than his head. He and his truck travelled toward the spot where Mom was working. Then, he crawled up on a chair so he could help.

"What are you doing?" asked Harvey.

"I'm wrapping a present for our friends. They're getting married, so we're having a shower for them."

Harvey said, "I think people should have a shower, so they will be clean for their wedding."

"This is a different kind of shower, Harvey. It's a shower of gifts." *I hope that the friends will not get hurt when the presents fall on them,* thought Harvey. "We're giving our friends things people need when they have their own home." Hearing that, Harvey slid down from the chair, and roared with his truck back to his room.

Mom finished wrapping the package and sat down at the kitchen table with a cup of coffee. She looked out the window at nothing in particular, and thought about the friends who were getting married. She prayed for their lasting love and faithfulness. In the middle of her silent prayer, Harvey dieseled back from his room.

"I have gifts for our friends," he announced, "things they need for their new home."

"Let's see what you have," Mom said as she looked down at a collection of odd bits in the bed of Harvey's truck.

Harvey picked up a picture of Jesus and handed it to his mom. "Everybody needs Jesus," he said.

"That's true, Harvey."

"I have Jesus in my heart, so I can give this Jesus to our friends."

"What else do you have, Harvey?"

Harvey handed his mother a fistful of dilapidated crayons, and half a bottle of bubbles. "Every home needs fun," Harvey explained. "These are fun things."

"And what's left in your truck?"

Harvey reached for the lint-covered piece of candy that had once been a valentine heart. "I found this in the bottom of my toy box," Harvey declared. "I'm going to give it to our friends. I want them to have love."

"You're right, Harvey, every home needs Jesus, and love, and fun."

And with that Harvey drove his truck back to his room, making truck sounds the whole way.

Help us to honor you in our home in all that we say and do.
John 13:34—35

64—WHO ARE WE?

Harvey was playing in his yard. He saw someone he hadn't seen before. Harvey had never met her, so he walked toward the girl. He didn't know what to say, so in a loud voice, he said, "I'm Harvey. H-A-R-V-E-Y." He looked at the new girl, and then asked, "Who are you?"

"I'm Pammy," she said, "Wanna play?"

Do you think Harvey and Pammy can be friends? What would help them to become friends?

Help us to show the kindness and love of Jesus to others.
1 Peter 2:1—5

65—KNOWING

Harvey went with Mom and Dad to the zoo. It was a cold day, so Harvey was all bundled up. His hood was up, an extra scarf was tied around his neck, and warm boots were on his feet.

Mom always said she liked to see the polar bears, so happy in the cold weather, so they watched the polar bears first. Harvey spotted the lion enclosure. He scampered ahead of Mom and Dad, and looked through the railing. The lion yawned, and Harvey cried out, "I'm a lion!" and yawned a big lion yawn.

Soon they came to the monkey mountain. Harvey loved the monkeys. There were so many! Monkeys were running, chasing, eating, swinging and resting. Harvey saw a mother and a baby. The mother moved quickly while the baby held on very tight. "I'm a monkey!" Harvey yelled, and grabbed Dad's leg, as tight as the little monkey was clinging to its mother.

Mom looked at Dad and smiled. Before long, they came to the penguin house and everybody was glad to go indoors, out of the cold. *The penguins are all dressed up*, thought Harvey. He watched them swim, and dive, and slide. He watched them walk. "I'm a penguin," Harvey said, and he began walking with stiff legs, like a penguin. He felt all black and white when he walked like a penguin. He was sure he *looked* like a penguin too. He walked back and forth. Then, he looked up to ask Mom and Dad if he looked like a penguin to them. He was surrounded by lots of legs, but none belonged to Mom or Dad. Harvey looked this way and that. *Where were they?*

"Young man, are you lost?" a kind person asked. Harvey

nodded. "Are you looking for your Mom or Dad?" Harvey nodded again. "What's your Dad's name?"

"Sometimes Mom calls him, 'Honey'."

The man smiled. Just then Harvey saw his dad. Dad reached out to him and said the best thing, "Harvey! That's my boy!"

Remind us today, Lord, that we are your people, created in your image.

Isaiah 43:1—7; Luke 3:15—22

66—Tempted

Harvey's friend, Pammy, was over for an afternoon of playing. In her regular voice, she said, "I'm the guest, so I get to decide what to play." Harvey did not think that was a rule at his house, but maybe it would be okay.

Then Pammy said in a bossy voice, "Let's play house. I want to play house. You be the baby. I'll be the mother." This was not Harvey's idea of having fun. He was not a baby. He did not want to act like a baby. He did not want Pammy for his mother, but he did not want to cause trouble, either.

Harvey lay down on the floor. He would try being a baby for his friend. Pammy laid a blanket over him. *That was okay*, he thought. Harvey lay there, trying to be the baby, but he began to make truck sounds.

"No, no!" Pammy said. "Babies do not make noises like that." Harvey did not want to cry, but he did not know any other sounds than crying that babies made. He was not having fun. Harvey stood up and saw that Penny had arranged all the little dishes on the table. Harvey said nothing, but he pushed all the dishes off the table. They clattered to the floor as Pammy squealed, "You wrecked it. You spoiled the lunch! It was all ready."

Just then Mom said, "It's time to do something else. Let's get out a game. I'll play with you."

When Pammy left with her mom, Harvey and his mom talked about the afternoon. "I didn't want to be a baby. I'm not a baby," Harvey said again.

"You aren't a baby, but a big boy like you shouldn't knock the dishes off the table, either," Mom suggested. "A person needs to be kind, even when he doesn't feel like it."

"I know, but playing house was no fun today."

Please help us to be kind even when we don't feel like it.
Luke 4:31—44

67—Healing

Harvey brought a handkerchief to his mother and said, "Please tie this around my head so my eyes are covered."

Mom fixed the handkerchief in place, just as Harvey said, "I'm going to pretend." Then he walked slowly around his house, feeling the chairs, and walls, and tables. He felt the floor. He felt the rug. He couldn't see anything. He walked into the next room and slowly moved around, feeling his way.

Then he fell down. This was not what he meant to do. "Help!" he cried. "Help! Help! Help!" Mom hurried to see what terrible thing must have happened.

"Help! Help!" Harvey called, too loudly for how close Mom was standing to him by then. "Help!" Mom took Harvey by the hand and pulled him to his feet. "Help!" Harvey called again.

"What is it, Harvey? What's wrong?"

"I can't see!"

"Oh! I thought you were hurt. Let's take off the handkerchief." Mom slid the blindfold off Harvey's eyes.

"I can see! I can see!" he squealed. And then he ran off to play somewhere else.

> *When we take our eyesight for granted, Lord, remind us that it is a gift from you.*
>
> Mark 8:22—26

68—PERFUME

Harvey and Mom had errands at the mall. They parked the car and hurried into the department store. Just inside the door, a lady was offering people perfume samples. "Would you care for a sample today?" the lady asked Mom.

"Oh, yes!" she answered, "This is *my* mom's favorite." She turned to Harvey. "It's Grandma's favorite," she explained, as the department store lady sprayed her wrist.

Harvey knew that the perfume smelled just like Grandma. He thought, *I could smell like Grandma too,* and he held up his hand for his own sample. Harvey breathed deeply. *It's Grandma's smell. Grandma always smells so good, just like this."*

Harvey imagined sitting in her lap and hearing a story. He could see her warm smile and hear her voice. Harvey thought about how much he loved Grandma and loved to remember the happy times they have had together.

Mom and Harvey hurried on their way, out of that store, and into the mall. Just then, Mom saw someone she knew, a lady doing errands with her boy. The moms started to talk and the boys looked at one another. Harvey didn't know this boy's name.

Then the boy said, "I smell something." He wiggled his nose, sniffing. "You stink," he announced. "You smell like a girl."

"I smell like my grandma," Harvey said importantly. "I like to smell like my grandma. She's the best."

Lord, let us carry your fragrance wherever we go. May it fill the house where we are, for Jesus's sake. Amen.
John 12:1—19

69—Being Alert

One day Harvey and his mom went to the home of one of mom's friends. The two moms sat at the table, planning and working together on something for church. Harvey did not have anything to do, so he kept hanging around. The other mom had an idea. She called her big boy and said, "Please get a paper and pencils and play tic-tac-toe with Harvey."

The big boy sighed and his shoulders drooped, but his mother looked at him with that look that made him know he had to do it, especially when she added, "Now," to what she said.

The big boy wrote "Harvey," "Me," and "Cat" on the paper, so he could keep the score. Harvey plopped down on the floor, took a pencil, and took his turn. He made Os when the big boy made Xs, but he did not win. Again and again the big boy made more Xs than Harvey made Os. Harvey did not like losing all the time. He went to his mom, pulled on her sleeve and whispered, "How can I win? I don't know what to do."

"Watch. Pay attention," she answered, and kept on talking with her friend.

Harvey tried some more. This time, he made Xs and the big boy made Os. Harvey put his nose close to the paper, watching carefully. He still could not beat the big boy. The big boy's name on the score sheet had a mark—lots of marks—for each game he had won. Harvey's name had no marks beside it. A tear started to come to his eye, and he did not want the big boy to see it. He went again to his mom. "I still can't win. I have zero wins," he whispered to her.

"Watch carefully. Keep an eye on the game."

That evening, Dad showed Harvey the secret of tic-tac-toe. He started by saying just what Mom had said that afternoon, "Watch carefully. Keep an eye on the game."

God, help us to pay attention. Let us see the important things, and live as you told us to, we pray.

Matthew 24:44

70—Thanksgiving's Over

Harvey went to church the Sunday after Thanksgiving. He wanted to talk about Thanksgiving. He wanted to talk about the wonderful day he had had with his cousins, but he looked around and saw nothing about Thanksgiving anymore. He did see candles, and tinsel, and a Christmas tree.

One of the grownups asked the children, "What are some of the things you are thankful for?" *Maybe he could talk about Thanksgiving!* thought Harvey as he listened.

Henry said, "Everything."

Polly said, "Mom and Dad."

Lou said, "Cousins."

Harvey looked around again at the Advent decorations. Then he said, "I am thankful for Jesus."

"Wow! I never thought of that!" Henry exclaimed softly.

"Me neither," whispered Polly, "but I wish that I had."

"When we see the decorations, and the candles, the gifts, and the lights, let's remember Jesus. Let's be thankful that Jesus came to earth to live among us and to die for our sins," the teacher told the children.

Thankful, yes, we are thankful for Jesus.
2 Corinthians 9:15; John 3:16

71—It's Coming!

Harvey and his dad were out doing errands. "Did you see that, Harvey?" Dad asked. "That flatbed was loaded with Christmas trees!"

"Christmas is coming!" Harvey said. He smiled, and said again softly to himself, "Christmas is coming!" He thought about Christmas trees. Soon there would be one in his living room. He thought about presents, and "Away in the Manger," and Baby Jesus. He thought about Christmas cookies, and his mouth watered. He loved to bite the heads off gingerbread people. *When Christmas came he would be able to do that!*

Harvey and Dad stopped at the hardware store. Together, they found what they were looking for. Dad paid for it, and as Harvey and Dad started for the door, the cashier handed Harvey a little candy cane. "Christmas is coming!" Harvey told the cashier. "Thank you."

On the way home Harvey saw the flatbed again. People were busy unloading it and arranging the trees, so people could look at them, and pick out the one they liked best. "Christmas is coming!" Harvey said again. "Christmas is coming!"

> *Let our hearts be ready, Lord, for your coming, for Christmas.*
>
> Isaiah 9:2

72—Upside Down

Harvey was so happy about Christmas. The tree at his house stood tall, covered with lights and ornaments. Mom had set candles and greens in many places. Harvey even had a Christmas candle sitting on the table by his bed.

Harvey loved to look at the lights and tree. He lay under the tree and looked up through the branches. He stood on the couch so he could see if the tree looked different when he was that tall. He touched the packages. The packages were of all sizes and shapes, with many colors of wrapping paper and ribbon. There was one very big package. Harvey even found some very small packages. He hoped the biggest package was his, so he decided to find out. Mom was reading. He went to her and asked, "Mom, is that big package for me? I mean the really big one."

"We'll see, Harvey."

"There's a very little package. I hope that's not mine," Harvey said.

"I don't know, Harvey. They say that the best things come in small packages." That did not make sense to Harvey. *How could the best things be small?*

On the way back to the Christmas tree, Harvey stopped at the manger scene. He looked at the angels and shepherds. There were sheep. There was a cow, and a donkey. There were Mary, and Joseph, and Baby Jesus. *Baby Jesus is so tiny, so small.* Very carefully, Harvey picked up Baby Jesus. "Baby Jesus is very little," Harvey said. Extra carefully, he laid Jesus back down in the manger. *Maybe*

Mom was right. Maybe the best things do come in small packages, thought Harvey.

Then he put his head on the floor so he could look at the tree from between his legs. The Christmas tree looked like it was hanging from the ceiling when he did that. The whole world looked up side down!

> *When our way of thinking is upside down from yours, help*
> *us to understand and trust you, O God.*
>
> Micah 5:2

73—MORE

When Harvey's friend came to visit, he walked over to the Christmas tree. He looked at it from the bottom branches to the angel on the very top. Then he announced, "Our tree is bigger, and we have more decorations, *and* we have more presents."

Harvey felt awful. He knew they had a pretty tree, with bright decorations, and many packages under the tree. Even so, what his friend had said still made him feel bad.

When the afternoon of play was over, and Harvey's friend had gone home, Mom asked, "How did you feel when your friend talked about how big his tree is, and how many presents he has at his house?"

Harvey hung his head. "I didn't like it. He made me want more."

"Christmas isn't about the biggest tree, and the most decorations, and all the packages, Harvey. It's about Jesus and the joy that he gives us. Jesus gives more joy than we can imagine. That's what Jesus brings at Christmas, and it's what really matters."

Help us, Lord, to think about the joy you give instead of worrying about getting more stuff.

Isaiah 61:1—4, 8

74—GLORY

Harvey put on his pajamas. He looked like he was ready for bed, but he did something very special, but it was not going to bed. He and Mom and Dad drove to a place to look at something called "Living Nativity." Harvey knew what the manger scene at his house looked like, and it was not alive. The one they went to see was real, living! There were real angels singing. There were real sheep with the real shepherds. A cow stood nearby breathing out steamy clouds. The donkey let out a loud noise and kicked its heels in the air. Harvey had never seen anything like this. He looked very hard. He could see Baby Jesus's mother and Joseph. They were real, too. "That's Mary and Joseph," he said. Harvey stood on his tiptoes. He wanted to see Baby Jesus. He looked very carefully and he was quite sure that he could see him, wrapped up in his mother's arms. Mom, Dad, and Harvey stood together in the cold, just looking, for a long time. Other people came and went quietly. Harvey did not want to leave, but he was getting colder and colder. Dad turned to go, and so did Mom. Harvey kept looking as long as he could. "Goodbye, Baby Jesus. Goodbye, Mary and Joseph. Goodbye, shepherds. Goodby sheep and cow," he said as he looked over his shoulder, walking away, while also trying to keep up with Mom and Dad.

They got into the car. No one said anything. They turned toward home, still quiet.

"Everything was there except the glory," Harvey said. He looked at Mom. She was wiping her eyes. Dad cleared his throat. The car was very quiet.

Before you know it, Harvey was tucked into bed, still thinking about Baby Jesus in the manger.

> *You reach out to us in the Christ Child, O God. Let us respond by receiving your gifts of love and life.*
>
> Luke 2:8—15

75—Remembering Christmas

Harvey was talking with Mom and Dad about Christmas. "What did you like, Harvey? What did you like best?"

Harvey thought about the Christmas tree, about big packages and small ones. He was very glad that big box had turned out to be for him. He loved the present that came in the big box. Mom thought her little present was wonderful, but Harvey liked his much better.

"Having all the family together is always special," Mom said.

"The men enjoyed the food and football," Dad laughed.

"The dessert was best," Harvey declared, "but it's all gone. The tree is gone. The company is gone. The pretty packages are gone. Christmas is gone!"

"Most of Christmas is gone, Harvey. But the best part of Christmas is still here. Jesus is here. Jesus is with us. When the ribbons and lights, the packages, the company, the tree, and the dessert are gone, Jesus stays with us." Dad said.

"I want to remember that every day," said Mom.

Jesus, you promised to be with us always. That is the good news to remember.

Matthew 28:20b

76—Returning to the Ordinary

At Harvey's house the Christmas decorations came down. The angel came off the tree. The shiny ornaments went into their box. On the carpet, around the tree, lay a ring of pine needles. The pine needles were the reason Mom said that it was time to get the tree out of the house. That made Harvey sad. He had loved watching the lights and looking at all the ornaments. One night, he had even slept by the Christmas tree. But now everything was packed away for another year. No more Christmas for a whole year. That seemed like forever to Harvey. Harvey's house was back to ordinary life.

But when Harvey got to church on Sunday morning, he discovered that at Church it was still Christmas! He saw the tree with all its decorations, still in its place. He saw the crèche, with Mary and Joseph, and Baby Jesus. He saw the candles and greens in their places. Harvey smiled a very big smile. Someone said, "We should keep Christmas in our hearts all year." He looked at his tummy and imagined a Christmas tree inside. He wondered if it would tickle. *Christmas in our hearts all year,* thought Harvey.

Later, Dad would tell Harvey that that means remembering God's love to us in sending Jesus. It means loving Jesus with all our hearts, every day of the year, even when life is ordinary.

Help us to love Jesus with our whole heart, all year long.
Luke 2:22—40

Printed in the United States
By Bookmasters